The Devil's Workshop

Camino del Sol
A Latina and Latino Literary Series

The Devil's Workshop

Demetria Martínez

The University of Arizona Press
Tucson

First printing
The University of Arizona Press
© 2002 Demetria Martínez
All rights reserved

♾ This book is printed on acid-free, archival-quality paper.
Manufactured in the United States of America

07   06   05   04   03   02   6   5   4   3   2   1

Library of Congress Cataloging-in-Publication Data

Martínez, Demetria, 1960–
    The devil's workshop / Demetria Martínez.
        p. cm. – (Camino del sol)
    ISBN 0-8165-2196-4 (cloth : alk. paper) –
    ISBN 0-8165-2197-2 (pbk. : alk. paper)
    1. Hispanic American women—Poetry. I. Title. II. Series.
PS3563.A7333337 D4 2002
811'.54–dc21   2001004112

British Library Cataloguing-in-Publication Data
A catalogue record for this book is available from the
British Library.

Publication of this book is made possible in part by the proceeds of a
permanent endowment created with the assistance of a Challenge Grant
from the National Endowment for the Humanities, a federal agency.

Some of the poems in this volume were published previously in
Hayden's Ferry Review, *Smartish Pace*, and the anthology *Power Lines:
A Decade of Poetry from Chicago's Guild Complex* (Tía Chucha Press).
The author would like to thank the Tucson-Pima Arts Council
for awarding her the 1998 Fellowship Award for Poetry in the
Literary Arts category.

To the Sunflower Coalition.

And with gratitude, as always, to the William Joiner Center for the Study of War and Social Consequences, University of Massachusetts, Boston.

Blessings also to Leah Henriquez Ready, my teacher.

Idleness is the devil's workshop.
           —Ancient proverb

Contents

The Devil's Workshop

Last Words

Here it is, my book, my black
Box from the cockpit.

Tell me how—after the winds
Severed a wing—I flew on . . . then landed.

The Devil's Workshop

They were right,
Our mothers and all
Their mothers before them.
Idleness is the devil's workshop.
Instead of writing a poem, I am thinking
About writing a poem: about you, of all people,
Who drove my pen like a tanker onto the rocks
Of the Galapagos, who ordered my pen
To lift off when I most needed
To circle the runway. Read my
Rap sheet. I could not write
A straight line the years we
Were lovers, the years the
Devil made his most
Acclaimed paintings
Out of my spilt ink.

Birthday

I was born in the Year of the Rat.
Black lung from the incense
Of burning American flags.
First poems penned by
The rocket's red glare.
Math was simpler:
58,000 soldiers
And then there were none.
I was born in the Year of the Rat.
Thirty-eight years, a life
Still at half-staff.

I Don't Want Love

Not love, but something

That, when it loses its green,
Holds its form

Like ocotillo,
Long flutes of cactus

To build a ramada
At the threshold of my house.

My house, my home,
In my name.

When I love myself
As I loved you,

I will invite you in.

Loneliness

The kernels of my loneliness are too stubborn to grind
Down to blue meal in my great-grandma's metate,
Too muddy for a dog to drink from,
Too fast for a pill to tag and tame.
I cannot climb the stairs of it
Nor offer it to my father's loom.
Its strands are too ragged
To weave a rug to ease
The walk across these cold bricks.

My loneliness lacks a plot.

It has no place inside the stories my mother tells
About surviving an earthquake in Assisi.
It has no place inside stories grandma told
About ignoring sirens, playing solitaire, reciting
Her rosary behind blackened windows in Cairo
When her pilgrimage to the Holy Land erupted in war.

Once I shouted my loneliness down.
After my birth, I cried out to my father
From Albuquerque to Okinawa with the help
Of a ham radio and the Red Cross.

My lungs inflated like sails, distance was nothing.
I went everywhere, passed from lap to lap
Of women who kept their loneliness secret
Until it happened to me, like the day of my first bleeding.

Blessing Poem

for Benjamin Theodore

They say it comes from our Indian side:
The blue birth spot near the base
Of the spine that, with time, fades away.
Little glowworm, doctors bathed you
In ultraviolet rays to rid you of jaundice.
Your parents played Mozart in the truck
To hot-wire your cerebral cortex.
When you coo, I dream of you transposing
English to Spanish to Tewa and back again,
Praying in so many tongues that some
God would have to hear if not answer.
Sweet fruit pit, live inside the mystery
While you can. The world is garbed
In a bullet-proof vest. Your eyes are
Obsidian arrowheads aimed at no one.

Threads

At this age you start to wonder which proverbs apply.
You paint one wall only, bordello burgundy.
You welcome into your life a man who brings flowers, and
 fliers,
Calls to boycott a clothing store with sweatshops in Vietnam.
At this age you touch what little sanctity you can muster.
The yearning burns to do more, to do more by hand.
To thread your very life through a needle's eye.

Birth Song

for David Demetrio

Our name is as gold as the grain
Of the goddess Demeter, clear as the glass
Counter at grandpa Demetrio's meat market
In Albuquerque. We are all over the map,
The hunter and the gatherer at war in us.

No one was prepared for the news
Of you, freak storm, but that accent
Over the í in Martínez was a bolt
Of lightning, your mother pushing
At gusts of up to sixty miles an hour
Until your cry tumbled out like thunder.

Let sleep ferry you across the days.
Soon enough your life will crack
Open like a fortune cookie; inside,
Your name will appear, nothing more.
Not even your parents know our secret.
That our name, though given, must be earned.
We must dream our way into being.

La promesa

for Sonia (born and died May 26, 2000)

You floated with the majesty
Of a storm
Into life and into death.

We made a home
For you, but you carried off
The roof.
We cupped our hands,
But your sweet
Waters turned to ash.

You wreaked so much
Hope and havoc, hacking away
At our dead roots. We're wanderers
Again in clay and in ink, remaking
Our covenant: to become
The eye of the storm,
El ojo de dios.

There is no promised land.
But the promise is good.
You said you would
Come, and you did.
Huracán. Rainbow.
Palo verde twig
In the beak of a hummingbird.

Final Exams

Now it's our parents handing us
Report cards: mom and dad pass
Their first biopsies, with extra
Credit for lower cholesterol.

Mom calls Tucson, triumphant;
Tells her 40-year-old,
"You kids are stuck with me!"
Dad calls, solemn, the good marine,
Grateful that the children
Can't court-martial him
For bowls of *menudo*
At Barelas restaurant.

Still, the rules hold:
Exercise, greens,
And no red meat.
So when death dries
Her dishwater hands
On her apron and steps
Out on the porch to call
My parents in, they can look
Down from their tree house
And yell, "Not time yet! Not time!"

Deposition

You make a mockery of the word *pending*, and mocked,
It mocks me in turn. You cite Zen tales to prove time does not
Exist anyhow, so why not wait for you a few more months?
Then it will be as good as done, like a cake in the oven—as long
As I tiptoe around the edges of your life so it doesn't collapse.

You will never sign. Your one free hand is clapping.
And where you hear music or silence, I hear the cry of a
    woman
Being pulled from the wrecked womb of a building in India.
It is a sin when I no longer know if I am weeping for another
Or for myself, if I am railing against a sleepy god who blinked
On his watch or a man, awake, who can't run out from
Under the swaying *vigas* of his own condemned house.

Remedios

Each cough is an underground nuclear explosion,
Unraveling your body's hard-won peace accord.
It's back to the bargaining table: garlic, C, zinc,
Oshá root, a five-day course of antibiotics,
And a glow in the-dark vaporizer, UFO among the mists.

You quiet your mind, that well-stocked pond of opinion.
You meditate on your lungs, failed sails.
Herbs from Uruguay float in a teapot like lashes.
The package reassures: you are saving the rain forest
With each new bout of respiratory illness.

Your body starts a fever, a controlled burn.
You fear you will go up like Los Alamos,
But your brain is an underground lab,
Oblivious to the flames, busy with equations:
You are too sick to be in one place at one time,

Much less ten places at one time.
So when friends call, you say, "No."
No. No. No. No. Then you just let it ring.
Already you are shaking this thing.
Like the Mayas, you discover the Zero:

The Buddha-you the wind blows through.

Rules of Engagement

Today I was told that the words
War is bad
Make for
Bad poetry.
OK.
Then consider
This poem
Dispensable,
Depleted
As uranium,
A poor poem,
A colored poem,
Drafted,
But not finished,
Out on a missing
Limb.
Nothing
But a little ink
Shed in the killing
Fields of university
Writing workshops.

News Footage: Kosovo Refugee Woman

What was she
Thinking
When she
Painted
Her nails?
Did she
Water
Plants,
Dry dishes,
The day
The earth
Stopped
Circling
The sun,
Heaven's
Dance
Cancelled?

She is a
Beauty
Mark on a
Mountain now,
Under a knife
Of rain,
Night,
Dark as
A wine
Whose
Name

She cannot
Pronounce.

Upon Waking

for Amadou Diallo, shot 41 times by police officers
as he reached for his wallet, New York City, 1999

In a dream after your death I stood on the rocky
Shores of an island. Dark-skinned people, young
And old, pressed against boulders as helicopter
Gunships took aim. I cried out at a wall of wind:
"No, stop, they have histories!"—but it was too late.
The soldiers were acting in self-defense
Against the sudden move;
A people firing a round
Of stories that might
Have opened hearts
Locked down as the
Lids of caskets.

Cold Snap in Tucson

The temperature plummets to 80 degrees.
Polar winds pluck the city's sole gold
Leaf like a gray hair. You sniff sweaters
Stored in wicker, shop for winter
Squash, clean beans: abacus beads
That tracked the hours until October.
Now summer has laid down her arms,
Extended statehood to autumn,
Rejoined the family of seasons,
Each taking a turn at the wheel.
Road rage ceases. We place gloves
In our glove compartments, not guns;
Run yellows, not reds; hew
To the golden rule: give cuts
To the van bringing a holy family
From across the border. The driver
Is your neighbor. I am your neighbor.
Tonight you will see a glow-in-the-dark
Manger on my rooftop, my inn draped
With red chile lights. I will slip the key
To winter beneath a potted cactus,
Forget where it is. For weeks, months
The city will scour the sky for
A star, for a sign, for a convoy
Of clouds with its freight of snow.

Not by the Gun but by the Grant Application

for the Southern Arizona People's Law Center,
10th anniversary celebration, Spring 2000

Not by the gun but by the grant application,
Which was due at midnight.
You stare at your screen as if through
A windshield at a body mangled beyond recognition.
You are not amused when I say that Che
Would have hired a computer tutor.
Go ahead, blame me for dawdling
Over your shoulder, a ballpoint poet
Who should stick with her day job.
Blame the full moon for popping
And gumming up the works
Like a modern-day Luddite,
Go ahead, rage against the machine.
I will write the goddam grant in sand.
Winds will overnight it to the Ford Foundation.
Fire ants will assemble each grain in plaintext
On the desk of a stunned bureaucrat who will
Write a check, only too happy to divest himself
Of dollars that this plague might pass over.
Peace will spread like shade over Tucson
Where we will sell *horchata* on the sidewalk,
Those quarters in the coffee can, the keys
That turn the water back on, the lights back on.
Come the monsoon the sky will spit diamonds
On the repaired roofs of your clients.
For this grant cycle at least, the letter
And the spirit of the law will be one.

Even the judges will disrobe.
There will be dancing in the halls of justice.

Insomnia

You should be sleeping the sleep of the dead.
You set out melatonin tablets like land mines,
But your monkey mind leaps over each one.

You try acupuncture, meditation, confession.
You sprinkle the bed with miracle dust from Chimayo,
Chicana feng shui, the TV sheeted in purple like Lent.

It occurs to you to read *The Complete Book of Needlework*.
Ten pages and your eyes close like hibiscus blossoms
Until the needle of wakefulness pricks your dreams.

The noises in your head are shrimp scuttling along
The ocean floor, filth eaters, radiant with half-life.
Already your day is dying like a coral reef.

Untitled

for J.

Like trying to capture
Lightning in a jar:
This poem about you.
Or pointing a wood
Flute at the sky
To channel the wind.

How easy it was when
I thought I knew
The nature of love.
Words flew from
My fingers in flocks.

All that I was sure of
Is burning like a village.
I can no more describe love
Than mystics can light.

You tell me to count my tears.
But by autumn they'd turned
Into eighth notes
And quarter notes,

A composition that never
Saw the stage, that with
Luck lives in the throat
Of a swallow nesting
After a war in a crumbling

Cathedral, a still-smoldering
But open door, this poem

For you, sweetheart, for you.

Flight

for Daisy

A man changes imperceptibly as the climate.
You find yourself grateful
For 102-degree days,
Yet dreaming of a cool
Rain for the sake
Of the children.

It is not to be.
Words fall from your
Husband's mouth like dry lightning.
You have never known a season like this one.
Exclamation marks strike acre upon acre.
Third-degree burns cover half
Of love's body—and you know
Whose body it is.

No choice now but emergency
Evacuation, the black belt
Of a road leading out,
The children and a suitcase
Behind night's tinted glass,
Itinerary in free verse.
The plane lifts off
The Managua runway,
Into a bloodshot sky.
You press this moment back
Like the page of a book.
The past is turbulence,

Shifting during flight.
The future? The future
Is unbraiding: Imagine
Wearing it any way you like.

Interlude

Don't bother, I did it
First. Broke my own
Damn heart. The better
To let you in. Diamonds,
Gold, go baby go, gut
Mt. Everest. Arrange
Me like flowers on
Flowered sheets.
Photograph me with
Your favorite knives.
We'll quit when
Our canary dies.
In three days you've
Slit everything but
My wrists. My turn
To level. Better watch
Your back. Bastard.
This ink is permanent.

Interlude #2

Day dying in the teeth of sunset.
A house ringed by sunflowers.
Sleep lost like rain forest.
Love? Devalued as a peso.

I'm the one Spanish word
You forgot to look up
That might have given meaning
To your life sentence.

Can you know how it was,
Driving in the dark to Albuquerque,
Each telephone pole
A crucifixion?

Her Ghost

Sometimes sits on the edge
Of the bed.
You loosen your grip
On me
And I touch the
Ledge
Overlooking your fractured history.

You see none
Of this.
You divide up the world
And metro
Sections
Of the newspaper.
We talk events, polish
Them with our
Opinions
Until they shine

But our moment?
Our
Moment
Died
In the dark
Without even a line.

Retro

I thought they were done
With this discussion in the 1960s:
Get your revolution
Out of my house,
It's pissing all
Over the floor.
Your holiness:
Living on rice and tea
For the sake
Of the hungry,
Juggling theories
To cure intellectuals
Of their apathy.

Remember me?
I could use a loving word,
A loaf of bread, a rose,
Help with the laundry.

Tell Me

Do you know who I am? If I fell to pieces could you
Reassemble the jigsaw? Do you know where it all
Goes: Grandma's prayer book, my cassette tape
Of Taos drummers, the postcard from El Salvador?

You—who've never even asked about my book
Of matches, to light the light I've carried
Through a hundred tunnels because
The light at the end is never enough.

The night is a boarded-up city of nameless streets.
Winds hiss through the slit tire of a star
While that other woman named Sleep
Holds you as I look on until morning.

Through a Needle's Eye

He who blasphemes against the Holy Spirit will not be forgiven.
—Luke, 12:10

He says at last he'll leave her, but his green
And gold words grow thin and drop, and here
It is winter, your spirit twisting out of you
Like piñon smoke from a chimney.
True believer, you take one more sip,
Sure as an alcoholic, swearing this time
The outcome will be different.

At age 35 you've run out of quarters
To telephone friends with your tale of woe.
As it is, their collective wisdom is a book
You dust and display but do not read.
Each day you become more articulate
About why you did what you did, much as
Some serial killers flanked by TV cameras.
Your friends love you, but they know better;
Know better than to believe you've
Seen the light you so love to describe.

Should your spirit return, you will know it
By the words that smolder
In your belly: tend the fire, count
On nothing except the alphabet.
Throw it like dice, fifty–fifty chance
The right word will come up.
This gamble is no game, this crack

At salvation, this making poetry
Out of what you nearly destroyed.

Snapshot, Tempe, Arizona

Tic-tac-toe of lightning.
Ornamental orange trees
From Vietnam in bloom.
Worlds tumbling dry
On a TV screen in
A smoke-free room.

The next morning,
You, going, gone.
Love, empty as the
Chamber of a gun.
Hole in my heart
Like a Chinese coin.

Abortion

For your sacrifice, no sacrament.
Even the Aztecs had priests at the cutting
Away of the heart, to pray for night to part.

Every anniversary, my friend, you will cry.
Your children and grandchildren will not know why.
The sun continues its walk across the sky.

Lessons

I would burn
Your letters
But that would be
Too cliché,
And there's not
One cliché
In any of them.
So I'll give the
Pages a hot
Soak in the sink,
Ink to oil slick.
Words I once
Skated across
Toward you,
Toward me.

Class Action

New York, Oaxaca: you promised trips.
For years I worked the late shift in your
Heart's sweatshop, assembling

Parts that make love tick.
Not even a raise, much less a union.
Rumors of a strike and you knock

At my screen door bearing fine
Wine, but my hurt is too vast
To fit inside a bottle like a ship

Where you are still at the helm,
Too proud to ask directions,
This time promising India:

Hennas and mantras,
Saris and tablas . . .
Sweetheart, I'll have to pass

On nirvana. I've seen so much
Light I need sunglasses.
The other huarache

Has dropped.
The redwood you hear falling
In the forest is you.

You Didn't Believe Me

When I told you about the other man
Any more than you believed
The day I announced that the moon

Was created when a swath of earth's
Mantle was shorn away in a cataclysm,
An asteroid, you don't believe

In cataclysms, don't believe me
Capable of discovery, of publishing
The very first paper, a new day opening like a switchblade.

I did it, the skeptics crucified me.
Baby, I turned the doorknob like a telescope
And walked into another man's room.

La tristeza

A German shepherd, a sewing machine, a beaded
Earring, Frida Kahlo's eyebrows: the clouds transform
   themselves
As they pass between two saguaros outside an office window
Where champions of justice beat their plowshares into swords.
Why fight the enemy when we can fight one another?
We build borders while the clouds bend them.

Another Way to End a Relationship

If you can't pull it up
By the roots,

Take it out

Of the sun, stop
Watering it.

Song

I dreamed my voice was an Anasazi pot
Filled with Tewa, Ladino, and Nahuatl.
The conquistadores crushed it when
They heard its savage sounds.
My songs and prayers bled into the ground.
And when the West was won and paved,
The topsoil, with all my words, blew away.

Seven shards of pottery were all I could find.
I strung them together, a wind chime.
I am mute, but the breeze is strong.
Oh sad, triumphant, beautiful song.
My sad, triumphant, beautiful song.

Needles

You're playing your veins
Again like harp strings.
Not even your family's
Shouts can be heard above
The rhapsody, the cooing
Of fanged cherubs.
On a good night you
Throw on a robe, call
The world to order
With a bottle, justice
That defies those who
Would restore you to
Some semblance of
Original beauty;
Your face full as fruit
· In a Frida Kahlo painting.

But the last thing you need
Is the same old advice.
You know how to braid
Desire the thickness of a
Phone cord, how to scale
Your prison walls when
Your moods change
Shifts like guards.
Look at the routes
Etched into your palm.
Steal the sweater that
Death is knitting

For you and run.
You will be captured
And acquitted. You will
Be sentenced to live.

Psalm

Damn the brain's chemical spills, evacuating
Every thought. Damn the smiles I pinned
To my face like a politician, a face
Like coffee with too much cream
Because I could not draw the
Curtain strings, raise the
Flag of a new day.
Cry, too, for the lost nights,
The poems, aborted, because I locked
The canvas of my heart in a man's closet
And talked my way into his bed.

I was nineteen when I saw the light
Of God escape like steam
From every living thing.
Now doctors say it was just
A tap dance of neurotransmitters.
But I know what I saw and what I heard:
How His heart pumped inside the heart
Of the Sandia Mountains like an accordion.

God, you alone know I took notes;
You alone know I wrote pages
And pages of psalms,
Then lost them on the road
Down a red-ribbed mesa north of Albuquerque.

Twenty years later I am rewriting them,
Remembering, dismembering.

God, will You forgive me
If I call them
Poems?

After a Reading in Arizona, the Author Is Detained by the U.S. Border Patrol in Las Cruces, New Mexico

for Roberto Rodriguez

They are doing exploratory surgery
On your car again—hubcaps

Gouged out again, canines
Sniff at empty sockets.

Oh, but the trunk—books
Lined in boxes like bullets,

Pages of Chicano history
To roll and smoke,

Ballpoint pens to shoot
Up with, red and black

Ink ruining our youth.
Handcuffed, you ask for water

But the Big Dipper has run dry.
Even Orion has drawn

Shut his curtain of clouds.
Only Night, with her

Badge of a moon, weeps,
Helpless to hide midnight's children.

El milagro

Sometimes when
I can't recall
An English word,
La palabra llega
En español.
It flies from
The crests of the
Sangre de Cristos,
Falls like roses
In winter from
Guadalupe's *tilma.*
I mean, how else
To explain
This miracle
When you've
Outgrown
The story
Of the stork?

The Decision Not

My biological clock ticks, but all that talks
Are words, herds of them, hordes, hives, schools,
Tools caked with fertile earth for the work ahead.

The said and the unsaid:
Two atoms flowering,
Powering peace.

A found poem,
A sound poem,
Oy veying, ay ay aying,

At one with the sighs
On the streets,
Blues and reds,

Yellows and greens
At one with the seen
And the unseen.

You and me,
Our treaty,
Poetry.

You Know Who

You were the best mistake
I ever made: my sweet
Spilt milk, my nation-state.

Three nights riding the lip
Of your San Andreas Fault.

Three nights until my head rolled
Like those Olmec busts
Carved of basalt.

Now it's back to my Mesoamerica
To discover myself.

So have at me, loot me while you can.
Then launch me like a satellite,
Unmanned.

Ars Poetica

(a found poem, from a flier at a Tucson *taquería*)

Concrete
Done
With
Quality
And
Honor

20 Years' Experience

Slabs
Sidewalks
Driveways
Garages
Exposed Aggregates

Big or Small

I'll Take It!

At a Kentucky Derby Party, Tucson, Arizona

Chatting with a Chicano author
Who is gay, we make the
Obligatory sign
Of the cross,
Utter: God forbid.

When my mother dies, he says,
Maybe then I can really
Write about sex.

May she live forever, I say.
But I know what you mean.
And I'm straight.

We sip mint juleps and wonder
How it would be to tear
The ticket of our
Imaginations
In two, good for
The X-rated matinee

Where we strip,
Unhook, unzip
On the big-screen
Computer: print
Our lives out,
Shake it all up,
Pop open the lid . . .

What tales
Would we tell,
God forbid?

Shyness (After a 20-Year Hiatus)

These days it is harder and harder
To speak.

The words are fleeing south
From heart
To hands.

Risking death by exposure
On the desert
Of the page.

Magic Wand

It's not what you write in the throes,
When a man has flown you like a kite.
It's what you write when you're lost,
Like the hiker who, for days, ate snow.

She remembered the mascara in her
Knapsack, and on a paper scrap,
Wrote her fiancé a last brief
Something about eternal love.

I confess to wondering why anyone
Would take mascara along on a hike.
But that is beside the point, a greater
Wisdom was surely at play.

Wiser than Kerouac at his typewriter,
Sucking words from a well as if
They were infinite—which they are not,
As our snow-eater no doubt knew.

Nothing Kerouac disgorged under
The influence came close to one woman's
Eternal love note, each word picked
For the life it would give, like her

Last ounces of raisins and nuts.
When rescuers arrived, they found
A woman, upright, blinking back ink,
Signing her name in the snow.

Rear Views

for Rachel Dolores

She used to drive
Me crazy. my mother
In the rearview mirror,
Donning her Avon lipstick
Before easing out of the driveway.
I was five years old.
I was in a rush
To arrive.
Ernie Pyle Library,
The children's room,
Where books smelled like
A forest after a storm.
I sat on the floor,
Enlightenment came easy.
If not, there was always
The card catalog, tarot
Of titles.

I'm older now, in no
Rush to arrive.
I, too, feel naked
Without my lipstick,
Without a book to open
Like a Japanese screen,
Behind which I rest, dream,
And rise, then read
Some more until
You arrive.

Upon Waking, a Lenten Dream

I walk to the front of the synagogue, take a seat.
(You cross your arms, stay standing in back.)
The congregants line up, come forward.
A rabbi smudges a circle of ash on each forehead.
I am thinking: I already received ashes on Wednesday.
I am thinking: I didn't know the Jews had such a ceremony.
I am thinking: Why am I surprised? So much of what we
   imagine
We invented was in fact inherited from the Jews.
Then a cantor, a woman, approaches me.
She opens a tin of honey, holds out the lid.
"Taste," she says, and I touch the gold liquid, touch my tongue.
Before she moves on, she says, "You must learn
To accept sweetness as you have accepted ashes."
(And you? As always you stand, detached.
Evading. Avoiding. The honey. The ash.)

Another White Man Goes Numb

Sisters, beware
The champion
Of colored folk
Who fucks then
Tucks your colored
Self like petals
Between pages
Of Karl Marx.

Sisters, beware
The man who
Would change
The world
For you
But not be
Changed
By you.
Who smokes
The opium of
Stale ideas
Year in, year out.

You *are* the people. You light candles to the santos then make
Your pilgrimage to the border to pray for the healing of the
     wound.

He does not eat grapes. He lowers himself into you, primitive,
     savage beauty.
The mere concept of you is enough to make him come. And go.

You *are* the people. Woman. *Mujer.* Not a flower. Not a fiction. He has fled to colder regions. Where you do not belong.

Accounts

One chopstick?
One oar?
What I counted
As gifts!
Hunger, drift.
Just like a woman,
Calling it love:
This low-intensity war . . .
Mistaking
A half-closed
For a half-open
Door.

The Word Heart

Is the cradle of
Art,
Heat,
Eat,
Hear,
Earth,
Ear . . .

But when I
Peer
Into the
Beveled
Mirror
Of my own
Heart,
All that is
There
Is the word
Tear
Traced
In sand.

No man's land.

The Wall

I should have read
My own poems.
They litter the landscape
Like monuments to the fallen,
Mortar of metaphor, cold
To the touch.
In the polished granite
A reflection
Of a flowering branch,
For years seducing
The eye . . .
I could not see
Our own names there
In the bricks,
Inscribed.

Junk Mail

I am waiting
For hope
To arrive
Like a circular
For a missing
Child. A face
Fast-forwarded
By computer,
Factoring in
The passage
Of time.

Here is how our love
Would look, years later,
If you still were mine.

Ki

You courted me
With the art of Japanese
Sword fighting,
Biographies
Of Che.

Then looked the other way.

You taught me well.
I stepped in, with
One strike split
Your mask
In two.

One woman's revolution:
To breathe
In the
Spirit
I once
Breathed
Into you.

Clock

for George Evans

Wear a watch
That does not work.
Because minutes lie,
Because hours are nails
In the heart of God.
Let the hands of time
Tame you instead.
Fingers of shadow,
Fingers of light.
The sun sets sail.
The sun docks.
Time is scrawled
On the sidewalk.
Open the curtain.
Look in on your life
Against the laughter
Of eternity.
Are you reading?
Are you weeping?
Are you setting out
A blue bowl of fruit?
Holiness flowers in
The fissures of this day.
Steep the seconds
Like manzanilla.
Wrap yourself
In the steam
Of centuries.

Take time's pulse,
Hot, in your own hands.

About the Author

Demetria Martínez is the author of two collections of poetry, *Breathing Between the Lines* (University of Arizona Press) and *Turning*, a manuscript that appears in an anthology of three Chicana poets titled *Three Times a Woman* (Bilingual Review Press). She is also the author of the novel *Mother Tongue* (Ballantine), winner of the 1994 Western States Book Award for fiction. The novel is based in part on her 1987 federal indictment on charges related to smuggling refugees into the United States, charges that carried a 25-year prison sentence. She was subsequently tried and acquitted on First Amendment grounds. Martínez is an activist with the Arizona Border Rights Project, which, among other things, monitors the militarization of the U.S.-Mexico border and documents abuses by the U.S. Border Patrol. She also writes a column for the *National Catholic Reporter*. Born in Albuquerque, New Mexico, Martínez received her B.A. from the Woodrow Wilson School of Public and International Affairs at Princeton University. She now resides in Tucson, Arizona.